INDIGENOUS PERSPECTIVE TO CLIMATE AND ENVIRONMENT

INDIGENOUS PERSPECTIVE TO CLIMATE AND ENVIRONMENT

Darren Parry

THE UNIVERSITY OF UTAH PRESS
Salt Lake City

Publication of this edition is made possible in part by The Wallace Stegner Center for Land, Resources and the Environment, S. J. Quinney College of Law and by The Tanner Trust Fund, Special Collections Department, J. Willard Marriott Library

This lecture was originally delivered on March 16, 2023, at the 28th annual symposium of the Wallace Stegner Center for Land, Resources and the Environment. The symposium is supported by the R. Harold Burton Foundation, the founding and lead donor since 1996, and by the Cultural Vision Fund and The Nature Conservancy.

The Defiance House Man colophon is a registered trademark of the University of Utah Press. It is based on a four-foot-tall Ancient Puebloan pictograph (late PIII) near Glen Canyon, Utah.

LIBRARY OF CONGRESS CATALOGING-IN-PUBLICATION DATA
Names: Parry, Darren, author. | University of Utah. Wallace Stegner Center for Land, Resources and the Environment. Annual Symposium (28th : 2023 : Salt Lake City, Utah)
Title: Indigenous perspective to climate and environment / Darren Parry.
Identifiers: LCCN 2023049694 | ISBN 9781647691806 (paperback) | ISBN 9781647691813 (ebook)
Subjects: LCSH: Ethnoecology—North America. | Traditional ecological knowledge—North America. | Environmental management—North America. | Indian philosophy—North America. | Philosophy of nature—North America.
Classification: LCC GF501 .P37 2023 | DDC 304.2/808997073—dc23/eng/20231122
LC record available at https://lccn.loc.gov/2023049694

Cover image: *Sunset at the Bear River Migratory Bird Refuge Tour Route* by Sandra Uecker\USFWS. Used under PDM 1.0 DEED.

Errata and further information on this and other titles available at UofUpress.com

Printed and bound in the United States of America.

FOREWORD

The Wallace Stegner Lecture serves as a public forum for addressing the critical environmental issues that confront society. Conceived in 2009 on the centennial of Wallace Stegner's birth, the lecture honors the Pulitzer Prize–winning author, educator, and conservationist by bringing a prominent scholar, public official, advocate, or spokesperson to the University of Utah with the aim of informing and promoting public dialogue over the relationship between humankind and the natural world. The lecture is delivered in connection with the Wallace Stegner Center's annual symposium and published by the University of Utah Press to ensure broad distribution. Just as Wallace Stegner envisioned a more just and sustainable world, the lecture acknowledges Stegner's enduring conservation legacy by giving voice to "the geography of hope" that he evoked so eloquently throughout his distinguished career.

Robert B. Keiter, Director
WALLACE STEGNER CENTER FOR LAND,
RESOURCES AND THE ENVIRONMENT

Centuries ago, the smoke of his wigwam and the fires from his council meetings rose in every village. The young listened to the songs and the tales of bygone years; they listened and learned, so that someday they might also repeat the same. The mothers took time out to play with their children and taught them to love and to appreciate the simplest joys of nature and life. The aged sat down with only memories of hunting, killing, feasting, starving and worshipping.

Braver men never lived than the Red Man, truer men never walked this land. They had courage, fortitude, and perseverance. They shrank from no danger and feared no hardship; fear, danger, and death were daily companions.

They were taught to love each other and to be united in all things and to be thankful for all favors they received. They dared not pluck a flower, twig, and herb or fruit unless they asked permission of the Great Spirit through prayer.

Little by little the Indian is vanishing—vanishing into the society of what you call civilization. He is trying to forget the wrongs done to him and his forefathers. He is trying to forget that once his forefathers owned this great land; that their seat extended from the rising sun to the setting sun. In memory, he can always recall the hunting of the buffalo, the deer, and other animals and fowls; that these creatures were made for his use by the Great Spirit. He can remember that Mother Earth was created to produce corn and plants for human use.

He must try to forget the day when white men crossed the great blue waters and landed on his land. He must remember that his forefathers were friends to the new people and not enemies. He must remember that he gave them a small seat.

He must remember that his forefathers gave them corn and meat. He must forget that in return for his kindness, he was given poison.

He must remember the strangers calling him brother and must forget that they only wanted a larger seat. They wanted more land and water; they wanted the whole country.

He can only recall, with great sadness, when the pony soldiers gave his people warm blankets contaminated with smallpox. Thousands upon thousands of Indians died.

We must try to forget the wrong done to us and strive for better things.

The Indian has been forced to leave his home, leaving the ashes of his native hearth. No longer does he see the smoke curl around his wigwam. No longer does he stalk the deer and buffalo. No longer does he creep upon the fowls; no longer is he going up and down the streams looking for fish. Now he is told that he has to have a license.

No longer is his chant heard at night. No longer are loud wails heard at death. He must express himself in a different manner. He has to wear shoes upon his feet—feet that would rather roam in soft skins. He must cut his hair because that is the way of a "civilized" man. He must wear his clothing even though his body cries for less of it. He must eat food that makes his teeth soft. His body and ways are slowly changing.

He is watching and waiting to see the effects of civilization upon men. Will civilization make them truer men, stronger men? The Indian is moving with a slow, unsteady step.

Before long he will catch the pace of the white man and move just as fast. But first of all, the Indian must erase deep resentments and painful recollections that are a distraction to him. Only in memory can he see the deserted villages and cast a glance upon the graves of his fathers and forefathers. He sheds no tears, utters no cries or groans. There is sadness in his heart that surpasses speech. He is looking forward and going onward.

But never for a moment is he going to forget that he is an Indian, a proud race born with a spirit that cannot be enslaved. Although his ways may change, his looks and thoughts will always be that of an Indian.

Just over a century ago the Colorado River Commission signed the Colorado River Compact at Bishop's Lodge in Santa Fe, New Mexico. The commission included delegates from the seven Colorado River Basin states and was chaired by Herbert Hoover. Do you know who was not there? The more than thirty federally recognized Indian tribes from the Colorado River Basin. Manifest Destiny was never about land in the West. It was always about water. Land without water rights is useless in the West. "First in time, first in right" became the law of the land. Unless you were Native American!

What if they had been invited to the table? Would things be different? Would the Colorado River, and many other waterways, be in the extreme crisis that they are in today if they were co-managed by Indigenous peoples?

We can begin to answer this question by pointing to work being done by my people on my traditional homelands. I am the former chairman of the Northwestern Band of the Shoshone Nation. One hundred and sixty years ago, some seven hundred members of the Shoshone nation were spending the winter, as they had done for centuries, near the Utah-Idaho border. Hot springs nearby provided a welcome place for them to catch their breath and catch up with friends and family during the cold winter months.

A half-mile to the east, Colonel Patrick Edward Connor and his 220 cavalry soldiers had a birds-eye view of the Shoshone encampment. In the early morning hours of January 29, 1863, they picked their way down a ravine toward the sleeping village and steaming waters.

Without so much as asking the Shoshone for the men believed to be guilty of attacking miners on the Montana Trail, the colonel and his men began to fire upon our people. Arrows were nothing compared to the rifles and sidearms of the soldiers. The soldiers began massacring men, women, and children. My grandmother said that our people were slaughtered like wild rabbits.

By early afternoon, more than four hundred of our people had died. Murdered at the hands of civilization.

In 2018, we were able to purchase 550 acres of the sacred burial ground known as the Bear River Massacre Site. This is only the beginning of a journey that began more than a century and a half ago to tell our story from our unique perspective.

My first visit after this purchase was to Utah State University (USU) where I met with professors from the College of Natural Resources. I told them my goal was to restore the land to what it would have looked like in 1863, using my grandmother's plant diary as a guide. Since I didn't possess the skill set necessary to make those kinds of decisions, I wanted to know if it was feasible. Our first interaction more than four years ago led to a collaboration that we enjoy today.

We have developed Shoshone partnerships with the science communities at USU and the University of Utah, as well as with other individuals and organizations. The vision is to create at the massacre site a living classroom. Doing so will require more than removing nonnative plants and trees and planting new seeds. It involves restoring the watershed, which will require buy-in from our neighbors upstream. How will they feel about the reintroduction of beaver into the ecosystem? How will they feel about changing their decades-old farming practices and creating riparian buffer zones? We will be moving Beaver Creek back into its original channel with the goal of reintroducing the Bonneville Cutthroat Trout. This is not a project that we can do alone. Healing begins when you can bring people together.

What we are doing at Bear River will symbolically and literally have a long-lasting impact on not only Bear River, but also on the future of Great Salt Lake and many other waterways. This type of Indigenous-led collaboration has the potential to restore landscapes and relationships across the western landscape.

I am thankful for the teachings of my people. Mountains are sacred, as they carry within their peaks and valleys the substances required to live—from the water running down the streams into our valleys, to the plants that were used as food and medicines, and to the animals we harvest to feed our families.

Slow down, listen, ponder the lessons that are being taught. There is a great natural order to the universe of which humans are an integral part. We are endowed with the ability to observe, learn, and imitate this order. It is a relationship of giving and taking. Of reciprocity.

I believe that ancient tribal cultures have important lessons for the world about the interconnectedness of all living things and our dependance on the natural world. We are damaging that world. Our environment and climate are changing.

Native people possess a profound spiritual kinship with nature. Pre-Columbus America was still our first Eden. Native peoples were transparent in the ecosphere. All of our decisions considered the effects of our actions on the generations to come. We do not live with that mindset anymore, but we need to start for our children, grandchildren, and those generations yet unborn.

When Columbus and others entered this continent, it bore the marks of thousands of years of human habitation and activity. As Europeans moved inland, they encountered settlements or recently abandoned agricultural landscapes. Assisted by Indian guides and subsisting on native food, the pioneers at the head of the Euro-American advance followed the signposts of cleared fields and orchards that have recorded the long experience of Native Americans in selecting good soils and managing local ecologies. But Europeans began to alter the landscape in ways that Native Americans had never done before.

Despite all of this, we have survived, and in some cases thrived. Our ability to adapt to the changing landscape has allowed us to still be here.

I want you to know that our languages are still strong, ceremonies conducted since the beginning of time still being held, and our governments still surviving. Most importantly, we continue to exist as a distinct group, as sovereign nations within the most powerful country in the world.

We have had a history that has contributed significantly to not just the United States, but to the world. There are not that many

Indians in the U.S. today and we tend to get overlooked in many ways. And when we are not being overlooked, we tend to get misrepresented. History, on occasion, has reduced my Native people to one-dimensional characters, important only in the sense that we taught the Pilgrims to grow corn.

We long to be heard and recognized. Our voices have been quiet for a long time and, in some cases, we are still searching for our identity. But we still have much to contribute.

We know that Earth and all of its creations came into being by the hands of a Great Spirit, as the designer and creator. The Great Spirit put into place finely tuned systems, cycles, and physical parameters that would always sustain life.

We were given careful instruction to take care of it. We are caretakers and not owners, a distinction that is often misunderstood today. The lands and water are not something to be bought or sold. They are a gift! The lands have always belonged to the Creator. We have been instructed to not overuse the land and allow it to rest during certain times. The Creator expects us to sustainably manage the resources that we have. We have been instructed to leave an inheritance for those yet to come.

The lands that colonizers first put their eyes on were not "untouched" or 'wild" as some have recorded, but rather the result of a broad range of Indigenous land management techniques.

In the late nineteenth century John Muir commented that the "Indians walk softly and hurt the landscape hardly more than a bird or squirrel." As a result, the land before the Europeans arrived was rich and fertile, organized and well-tended. Our people did not struggle against nature. They worked within set boundaries and out of a spirit of respect. We took no more than we could use and used all that we could from what we took, always making sure to put the time and energy back into the land so that it would continue to yield and continue to produce for generations to come.

We have always believed, as you should, that the Great Spirit put everything on this earth for our survival. Nature needs to be tended and carefully and lovingly maintained; to be respected and not dominated. The natural resources on this earth will continue to produce year after year, but only when our steps are light and our hearts are right.

But things have changed. How do we reconcile the past where Western values have taught us that "We have rights" and can use the land for extraction and depletion, versus Indigenous values that teach us that "We have obligations"? Obligations to the past, present, and future generations. Obligations to our communities.

Western world views are scientific and skeptical, often requiring proof as a basis of belief. Indigenous worldviews are based on a spiritually orientated society. This is a system based on belief in the spiritual world. To Native peoples, land and water are spiritual.

Western worldviews say that there is only one truth based on science or law. Indigenous worldviews say there can be many truths. Truths are dependent upon individual experiences.

Western worldviews have a way of compartmentalizing society. Indigenous worldviews say that societies operate in a state of relatedness. Everything and everyone is related. Identity always comes from connections.

Western worldviews say that the land and water and their resources should be available for development and extraction. Indigenous worldviews believe that the land and water are sacred and only given by our Creator to be carefully and lovingly cared for.

Western worldviews judge your success by how well you have achieved your goals. Indigenous worldviews judge success by the quality of your relationships with people.

Western worldviews say that human beings are the most important in the world. Indigenous worldviews say that human beings are not the most important in the world.

And Western worldviews teach that amassing wealth should always be for personal gain. Indigenous worldviews say that amassing wealth is important for the good of the community.

Do you know that the Iroquois Nation leadership does not make any decisions without considering what effect that decision will have on seven generations ahead? Think about the implications for the future if that was how our leaders governed.

There is an old Native American proverb that says, "We do not inherit the earth from our ancestors, we borrow it from our children." What kind of world are we leaving them? What will their world look like?

Scientist Gus Speth once said:

> I used to think that the top environmental problems were biodiversity loss, ecosystem collapse and climate change. I thought that with thirty years of good science we could address those problems. But I was wrong. The top environmental problems are selfishness, greed, and apathy, and to deal with those we need a spiritual and cultural transformation. And we scientists don't know how to do that.

But we have got to start making decisions that will allow our environments to heal.

What should these policies look like? We need policy to promote regenerative agricultural practices upstream and to support farmers and ranchers who are conserving water and improving the health of the soil. We can all be involved in organizing land restoration activities that build resiliency to drought. Restoring beaver habitat and the health of upper watershed riparian areas is a promising approach. The restoration efforts at Bear River are good examples of this and could serve as a model for restoration across the country. By using our water rights to restore Beaver Creek and riparian habitat along the Bear River, we are ensuring greater flows to the Great Salt Lake.

Proposed legislation is a start, but we need to stay organized and keep up the political pressure to get this and other legislation across the finish line. We are taking baby steps for a problem that will require leaps and bounds.

The elephant in the room, however, is future climate change. We must increase political pressure for climate legislation that immediately reduces greenhouse gas emissions. We have got to come to terms with our culture of consumption, extraction, and depletion.

Can this be done?

This past October I had the opportunity of giving a lecture in Copenhagen, Denmark, entitled "An Indigenous Perspective to Climate and Environment." It was well received. They entertained me for eight days, and every night I had the opportunity to go out to dinner with a different professor and five to ten students, and every night we talked. What I got out of sessions that went well into the night is that these people live those Indigenous values. They have less for the sake of the health and wellbeing of the community. They live sustainably. Their water and air are clean. They will be carbon neutral by 2025. They walk or bike everywhere. I asked them why they are listed as the happiest people in the world. Their answer was simple. We all have healthcare, we have a home to rest our heads, and we all have jobs. Why wouldn't we be happy?

We need to change our thinking and consider the health of not only the people but also the health of the watersheds that nourish our lakes and rivers and our nonhuman kinfolk. The health of the people will always parallel the health of our water and environment.

You see, scientists are finally discovering what Indigenous elders have been teaching for generations: that we are all connected. Politicians are finally discovering what the Iroquois already knew: that we must govern for the benefit of future generations. This is what the young activists are saying when they demand climate justice. We cannot sacrifice their future for the sake of short-term profits. "There is not enough science in the world that will overcome our selfish behaviors."

> One day a hunter brought home a sizable kill, far too much to be eaten by his family. mountain man asked how he would store the excess. Smoking and drying technologies were well known, so storing was possible. The hunter seemed puzzled by

the question . . . store the meat? Why would I do that? Instead,
he sent out an invitation to a great feast, and soon the whole
village had gathered around his fire and ate until every last
morsel was consumed. This seemed to puzzle the mountain
man who again asked, given the uncertainty of fresh meat in
the forest, why didn't you just store the meat for yourself and
your family? Store the meat, the hunter said? I store the meat
in the belly of my brother.

As we become successful by the world's standards, can I just
make one suggestion? I hope that our status in this life will be
determined not by how much we accumulate, but by how much
we give away and how much we do to serve in our individual
communities.

We know what to do. We know what the problem is. We know
the drivers of climate change. We know all of these things, yet we
fail to act. We fail to act because we haven't incorporated values
and knowledge together.

Now is the time to braid Indigenous and scientific knowledge
to manage our environment in ways that achieve our conservation
goals and also support Indigenous sovereignty. There are a growing
number of cases that illustrate how to operationalize this knowledge-
building in the context of Indigenous-led restoration efforts. Tribes
are leading out across this country and they are showing us how.

When you assume that scientific knowledge is superior to Indigenous wisdom, you make collaboration impossible. And that is
what we are going to need.

We are in the midst of a massive paradigm shift. Now is the time
to braid together Indigenous knowledge and values about our
stewardship with cutting edge biophysical science to create watershed institutions and create policy to steward our water and our
environment and climate for future generations.

The world as we know it has ended for many things, many times,
but in this era, this time, this now, is a never before known time to
create, to investigate, to listen, and to invent. Not because we have

the answers, not because we know the way, but precisely because we don't.

I do not know how to fix this alone. But I believe that abundance sprouts up in strangely improbable places. And what I do know is that I will be fighting alongside you, for many foreseeable years, and I hope you will too.

There is a certain poppy that gets its germination cues from smoke. After the devastating wildfires in California in 2019, the hills that were turned to ashes were now lined with those beautiful golden poppies. Similarly, we were born to bloom, not in spite of the fire in our lives, but because of the fire. Our creator needs a people on fire!

I love the prophecy of Chief Crazy Horse, who I believe could see our day and time, when he said this:

> Upon suffering beyond suffering, the Red Nation shall rise again and it shall be a blessing for a sick world. A world filled with broken promises, selfishness and separations. A world longing for light again. I see a time of seven generations. When all of the colors of mankind will gather under the sacred tree of life and the whole earth will become one circle again. In that day there will be those among the native peoples who will carry knowledge and understanding of unity among all living things, and the young white ones will come to those of my people and ask for this wisdom. I salute the light within your eyes, where the whole universe dwells. For when you are at that center within you, and I am at that place within me, we shall be as one.

I think the words of Crazy Horse are prophetic, like many Native American leaders who went before and will come again.

WE CARRY THIS LIGHT. LET US SHARE IT WITH YOU.

"What if this climate change talk is a big hoax and we end up creating a better world for nothing?" Think about that for a minute.

ABOUT THE AUTHOR

Darren Parry is the former chairman of the Northwestern Band of the Shoshone Nation. He teaches Native American history at Utah State University and serves on the board of directors for the American West Heritage Center, in Wellsville, Utah, the Utah Humanities board, and the PBS Utah board of directors.

DELIVERED AT THE 2023 WALLACE STEGNER SYMPOSIUM

COPUBLISHED WITH
The Wallace Stegner Center for Land, Resources and the Environment
and the J. Willard Marriott Library Special Collections Department

The American West encountered by European colonizers, far from being *untouched* or *wild*, has been shaped by a broad range of Indigenous land and water management techniques over thousands of years. Indigenous peoples continue to pass down traditional knowledge about the land and their relationship to it. The assumption among some today that western-based scientific knowledge is superior to Indigenous wisdom can be a barrier to meaningful and lasting collaboration. We must work together, merging traditional Indigenous and scientific knowledge, if we are to heal the land that we have collectively sullied. These ideas explored by Darren Parry culminate in a single, thought-provoking question about how to care for the Earth.

Darren Parry is the former chairman of the Northwestern Band of the Shoshone Nation. He teaches Native American history at Utah State University and serves on the board of directors of the American West Heritage Center in Wellsville, Utah; the Utah Humanities board; and the PBS Utah board of directors.

THE UNIVERSITY
OF UTAH PRESS
www.UofUpress.com

978-1-64769-180-6 $7.95

9 781647 691806   50795>

Cover image: *Sunset at the Bear River Migratory Bird Refuge Tour Route*
by Sandra Uecker\USFWS. Used under PDM 1.0 DEED.

GREAT SALT LAKE

A Perspective from the Church of Jesus Christ of Latter-day Saints

Bishop W. Christopher Waddell